ASSESSING EGYPTIAN PUBLIC SUPPORT FOR SECURITY CRACKDOWNS IN THE SINAI

Egypt has a serious security threat emanating from the Sinai Peninsula. Over the past several years, but especially since the ouster of Muslim Brotherhood President Mohammad Morsi in early-July 2013, the level of terrorist activity and violence against Egyptian security forces has escalated to high-levels. The violence threatens Egypt's stability and its ability to get its troubled economy to rebound, particularly over such important economic engines as tourism and foreign investment. Newly elected Egyptian President (and former Field Marshal) Abdel Fatah al-Sissi stated in his inaugural speech that, as president, stamping out terrorism is his first priority.[1] For the United States, the security problem in the Sinai has important ramifications as well. It threatens the stability of the most populous country in the Middle East region — a linchpin state in the area; it threatens the peace treaty between Egypt and Israel; it has the potential of a spill-over effect to threaten the vital Suez Canal waterway, upon which U.S. military ships (as well as merchant ships) pass from the Mediterranean to eastern Africa, the Arabian Sea, and the Persian Gulf.[2]

The Egyptian military, which has taken the lead in security operations in the Sinai, seems determined to use maximum force to pacify the Sinai and eliminate the threat posed by the terrorist groups. One of the key questions that has not been explored is: How much leeway, in terms of Egyptian public opinion, does the Egyptian military have in these security operations? In other words, to what extent does the Egyptian public give the Egyptian military wide berth to carry out such operations? Related to this question

1

is to what extent such operations can backfire and rebound against the Egyptian military and government if they are not successful? Furthermore, to what extent can such operations, because they employ so much violence and severely impact the lives of Bedouin villagers, create even more problems for the military and impact the attitudes of Egyptians concerned about the government's human rights abuses?

Characteristics of the Sinai and Its Complicated Image.

The Sinai Peninsula is a very complicated piece of territory. The western part straddles the important Suez Canal waterway, with the major cities of Port Said, Ismailiya, and Suez located on the western side of the canal. The southern tip of the Sinai includes the important resort areas of Sharm El-Shiekh and Ras Muhammad, which draw many thousands of European tourists every year and are an important source of revenue for the state. The town of Taba by the Israeli border and the Gulf of Aqaba in the southeastern portion of the Sinai traditionally has attracted Israeli and other foreign tourists. The central, northern, and eastern parts of the Sinai are mainly mountainous and desert areas inhabited by Bedouins who traditionally have been marginalized in Egyptian society. They have a reputation in mainland Egypt as a sort of lawless and rootless people who earn their living by smuggling and other nefarious activities.[3] Whether this characterization is justified or not, it seems to be widely held by the Egyptian people who inhabit the Nile region, that is, most of the population. Hence, in the eyes of most Egyptians, the Bedouins are not considered truly "Egyptian." They live on Egyptian territory but are not considered full citizens. For example, they are excluded and exempted from the military and the police services for complicated reasons, but in large part because their loyalty to the nation-state has always been suspect. Correspondingly, they have always received a much smaller share of state resources.[4] In addition, in the northeastern part of the Sinai, bordering the Gaza Strip, there is a small community of Palestinians who have been living there as refugees since the 1948 Arab-Israeli war.

As a kind of "wilderness area," most of the Sinai is largely unknown to the Egyptian public. It has never been a place where Egyptians from the Nile have settled, except for the development of the resort areas in and near Sharm El-Sheikh since the mid-1980s. Much of the peninsula has long been a closed military area, contributing to its rather mysterious and wilderness status.

This is not to say that the Egyptian people do not consider the Sinai as Egyptian territory. Indeed, when Israeli forces occupied the Sinai after the 1967 war, the peninsula's loss was seen as humiliating by the Egyptian people, a situation that needed to be rectified.[5] The Sinai is important strategically for Egypt because it is a "buffer zone" between Israel and "mainland" Egypt, and it gives mainland Egypt a kind of "strategic depth" in the face of invasions coming from the east (as proved to be the case when the Ottoman army invaded it in the early stages of World War I, and when the Israelis invaded it in 1956 and 1967). Former Egyptian president Anwar Sadat invested much time and energy trying to retrieve the Sinai through a combination of war and diplomacy. In the October 1973 war, the Egyptian military's successful crossing of the Suez Canal and the recovery of territory in the western part of the Sinai was seen as a great victory by the Egyptian people because they had finally gotten some of their lost lands back and had inflicted substantial military losses on the Israelis. Although the Israelis counterattacked, and the war was fought to a sort of draw, Egyptians still tout that war as a great victory after the humiliating defeat and the loss of the Sinai in 1967. Subsequent diplomatic efforts supported by the United States in the form of the Camp David Accords of 1978, and the Israeli-Egyptian peace treaty of 1979, enabled Egypt to retrieve all of the Sinai by 1982. Although Egypt was criticized by much of the Arab world for concluding a so-called "separate peace" with Israel, Sadat and most Egyptian citizens held the view that Egypt had made enormous sacrifices for the Palestinian and Arab cause since 1948, and no country had the right to criticize it for getting its lands back.[6]

One of the consequences of the Israeli occupation of the Sinai from 1967 to the early-1980s was that there were suspicions that many of the Bedouins in the Sinai had collaborated with the Israelis.[7] The Bedouin deny this charge, but the notion persists among many mainland Egyptians, and it may be one of the reasons why the Egyptian military continues to exclude the Bedouin from military service.

Another consequence of the Israeli occupation of the Sinai was that, as a price for peace and the return of the Sinai to Egyptian sovereignty (including oil resources there at the time), Cairo was compelled to accept military restrictions (concerning the amount of military equipment and troops) within various zones in the Sinai Peninsula. The Multinational Force and Observers (MFO) peacekeeping force, supported by the United States, has been monitoring this agreement since that time. Egyptian officials, and Egyptians with general knowledge of these restrictions, were never happy with this arrangement, but they grudgingly accepted it as the price to retrieve the Sinai. Periodically, there have been calls by some nationalist and Islamist political figures in Egypt to revise the terms of these military restrictions,[8] but nothing official has come of this because it would take the concurrence of the Israeli government to do so. Nonetheless, with the upsurge of violence by extremists in the Sinai since 2011, the Israelis and the Egyptian governments have come to behind-the-scenes agreements and understandings to allow more Egyptian military assets to be deployed to their common border than would otherwise be the case. It appears that the Israelis are generally accepting of the deployment of additional Egyptian military assets to the border, as they serve both countries' interests in seeing the Sinai pacified and tunnel activity from the Sinai into Gaza closed. One Israeli scholar, writing in January 2014, noted:

> Over the past year, Israel and Egypt have used little-known, legally permissible understanding—the Agreed Activities Mechanism—to bypass restrictions on the number and type of Egyptian forces permitted in much of the Sinai. In doing so, they have made de-facto modifications to their 1979 peace treaty without resorting to the diplomatically risky procedure of 'reviewing' the treaty itself. As a result, considerable Egyptian army forces are now constantly deployed in central and eastern Sinai (Areas B and C of the peninsula, respectively), in a manner and scope never envisioned by the teams that negotiated the treaty more than 3 decades ago.[9]

The only time the Israelis protested this increase in military assets was in August 2012 when the Egyptian military apparently did not inform the Israelis in

5

advance about the movement of military assets close to the border.[10] But this disagreement soon dissipated, and cooperation between the Egyptian and Israeli military and intelligence services reportedly has been working smoothly since that time, even during the presidency of Mohammad Morsi.[11]

Developments in the Sinai.

Prior to the 2011 revolution which led to the resignation of Hosni Mubarak as president, Egypt's main fight with terrorists occurred in the 1990s in the Egyptian mainland, when the Islamic Group *Al-Gamaa Al-Islamiyya* and the Egyptian *Islamic Jihad* undertook attacks against regime officials, policemen, and foreign tourists, hoping to weaken the state and somehow cause the regime to fall.[12] Although hundreds of Egyptians and scores of foreign tourists died over the course of the 1990s, the regime was able to defeat these terrorists through a combination of security measures, economic development in some neglected urban areas, as well as in rural areas of Upper Egypt, and effective propaganda. Perhaps more importantly, most Egyptians, while disliking the Mubarak regime, never saw these terrorist groups as viable alternatives to Mubarak's rule. Furthermore, the terrorists' tactics of attacking foreign tourists and policemen were seen as both "un-Egyptian" and "un-Islamic," for they only contributed to hurting Egypt's image abroad and putting hundreds of thousands of people involved in the tourist industry out of work.

After the September 11, 2001 (9/11) attacks by al-Qaeda against the United States, there appears to have been some extremists (whether Egyptian or foreign), perhaps affiliated with al-Qaeda, who came to the

Sinai to undertake terrorist acts against foreign tourists and Israeli targets. Although only a few of such attacks occurred between 2004 and 2006, the Egyptian military reacted strongly against them, especially since they occurred in the Sinai resort towns of Sharm El-Sheikh, Taba, and Dahab, which are important sources of foreign revenue. The Egyptian government claimed that the October 7, 2004, attack in Taba, which killed 34 and wounded 171, was undertaken by a Palestinian who had recruited some mainland Egyptians and Bedouins as accomplices. In the aftermath of this incident, the Egyptian government rounded up 2,400 people, the majority of whom were probably Bedouin, and kept many of them incarcerated for years.[13] Three purportedly mainland Egyptians were later sentenced to death.

Despite government claims that it either rounded up or killed the perpetrators of these attacks, the dragnet did not apparently capture all of the terrorists. More worrisome, these terrorists were able to continue to entice many disaffected Bedouin youths to join their ranks and inculcate them in Islamist extremist beliefs. At the same time, after Hamas took control of the Gaza Strip from Fatah in 2007 and Israel imposed a trade embargo on the area, tunnel digging—and the smuggling of goods, food, and weapons—became a very lucrative activity between the Sinai and the Gaza Strip. This smuggling activity was especially important for Hamas during and after the first of several mini-wars between the Hamas and Israel in 2008. Who actually dug the tunnels remains somewhat unclear (Palestinians or Bedouin), but certainly the terrorist groups, including Hamas, and some Bedouin tribesmen, benefitted substantially from the smuggling activity. As the smuggling business thrived, many Bedouin tribes became essentially armed gangs with military equipment, such as machine gun-mounted pickup trucks. Egyptian police forces soon proved to be no match for such armed groups.[14]

Developments since the 2011 Revolution.

During the Egyptian revolution of January-February 2011, thousands of inmates in Egyptian prisons were freed or freed themselves in the chaos that ensued when the police abandoned their posts. Included in this group were many terrorists, some of whom remained in mainland Egypt while others went to the Sinai. One of the prominent escapees was Ramzi Mawafi, a doctor who joined al-Qaeda in Afghanistan in the 1990s, but was subsequently arrested by Egyptian authorities. According to Egyptian security officials who spoke to the Associated Press, Mawafi is believed to be in the Sinai coordinating the terrorist groups and helping them secure money and weapons.[15] In the Sinai itself, the temporary "disappearance of the security state gave Sinai's population the opportunity to avenge its suffering by sacking abandoned checkpoints, police stations, and intelligence offices throughout the peninsula."[16] The Supreme Council of the Armed Forces (SCAF), which initially ruled Egypt after the revolution, tried to quell such activity in the Sinai, but with mixed results. SCAF put more troops into the Sinai to fill the security vacuum left by the ineffective police forces, but these troops were unable to pacify the area or prevent the gas pipeline from Egypt to Israel from being attacked several times. During 2011, the Bedouin tribesmen, probably in conjunction with extremist elements:

attacked the police station in al-Arish, orchestrated seven pipeline explosions, repeatedly disrupted traffic on the main road to the trade terminal with Israel, skirmished with Egyptian forces that have ventured into Wadi Amr and other Bedouin strongholds, and expanded their large-scale trade in organs harvested from African immigrants.[17]

Shortly after Mohammad Morsi of the Muslim Brotherhood won the presidency in the summer of 2012, a serious terrorist incident occurred in the Sinai. On August 5, 2012, a group of Islamist extremists fired on Egyptian soldiers in the Sinai border town of Rafah, killing 16 of them, stole their armored vehicles, and attempted to smash into the Israeli side of the border before being stopped by Israeli forces.[18] The incident was an embarrassment for the Egyptian military, and Morsi used it to reshuffle Egypt's military and intelligence services. Minister of Defense Hussein Tantawi and Army Chief of Staff Sami Annan (both of whom had opposed Morsi for political reasons) were sacked, as were the heads of air force and navy commands. Abdel Fatah al-Sissi, then head of military intelligence, was named Defense Minister. This reshuffling of the military hierarchy proved popular with the Egyptian people, some of which favored the removal of the SCAF old guard leadership because of the SCAF's repressive policies in the 2011-12 period,[19] while others believed that Egyptian soldiers should have been better protected against the extremists, and that the top brass should be held accountable.

Interestingly, shortly after this leadership shakeup, new Defense Minister al-Sissi traveled to the North Sinai on August 20, 2012, to meet with disaffected Bedouin tribal leaders to hear their complaints and to enlist their support against the extremists. Reportedly, al-Sissi offered rewards to the Bedouins to collect weapons in the area, and he promised that $165 million in development assistance would be sent to the region.[20] It is not known whether any weapons were collected or such assistance was ever rendered. Morsi himself promised economic development in the North Sinai, but this never materialized, according to one analyst, in part because of fiscal constraints and pressing needs in the Egyptian mainland.[21]

In early-July 2013, Morsi was ousted by al-Sissi and imprisoned after millions of Egyptians came out to protest his rule. Egypt's public prosecutor in May 2014 said that investigations of terrorist suspects showed that Morsi had struck a deal with the main terrorist group in the Sinai, *Ansar Beit al-Maqdis* (Supporters of Jerusalem), to refrain from attacks during his presidency in exchange for pardoning members of the group.[22] It is difficult to verify these charges. Morsi's public encouragement of Egyptians going to Syria to fight against the Assad regime, and the statement of one of his top aides that Egyptians who did so would not be prosecuted upon their return,[23] was probably a cause of concern for the Egyptian military and intelligence services who were worried about the returnees from such conflicts.

What is known is that after Morsi was overthrown, terrorist activity in Sinai increased markedly. Egyptian military and security services came under attack almost daily in the Sinai in the summer of 2013, replete with roadside bombs and executions of military personnel. The new, military-backed Egyptian government blamed the Muslim Brotherhood for these attacks and claimed that the Brotherhood not only had close ties to these terrorist groups in the Sinai, but were actively coordinating with them. One Brotherhood leader claimed that these attacks were in retaliation for the coup against Morsi.[24] Whether this statement was based on the actual situation, or was merely bravado meant to scare the military, is unknown, but it played into the Egyptian military's narrative that all of the terrorist violence was linked to the Brotherhood. One thoughtful analyst has written that:

> more likely, the increase in salafi jihadist attacks came from an opportunism on the part of the militants—who were not supporters of the Brotherhood while it was in power—and a response to a newly activist military in the [Sinai] peninsula: an increase in Egyptian military forces provided an increase in salafi jihadist targets.[25]

For its part, *Ansar Beit al-Maqdis* tried to capitalize on the government's severe crackdown on pro-Morsi supporters in mid-August 2013 by stating: "We were horrified by what they saw of massacres against the helpless Muslim masses."[26]

Terrorist Groups in the Sinai.

The extremist elements in the Sinai are made up of several groups, perhaps with membership numbering about 1,600,[27] the most prominent being *Ansar Beit al-Maqdis* who probably came into being in 2011. Membership in this organization is somewhat murky, but it is believed to consist mostly of Egyptian nationals, some of whom, including a few former Egyptian army officers, had fought with Islamist extremist forces in the Syrian civil war, plus a smattering of foreign Arabs who have come to the Sinai after having fought in Syria and other conflict areas. The group claimed responsibility for the August 2011 rocket attacks on

Eilat, Israel, near Egypt's Sinai border with Israel, during which 13 Israelis were killed. In October 2011, al-Qaeda leader Ayman Zawahiri praised this operation and added that one of its gains was:

> exposing the treason of the ruling [Egyptian] military council, which was quick to send it troops to chase [Ansar operatives] in order to protect Israel's security, and then begging from Israel to increase the forces in the area so as to pursue Israel's enemies.[28]

One press report noted that *Ansar Beit al-Maqdis* has shown:

> it can build and remotely detonate large bombs in strategic locations, gather intelligence about the precise timing of movements by their targets, record their own attacks and manage the complicated maintenance of an advanced portable surface-to-air missile—all suggesting combat experience.[29]

Interestingly, both al-Qaeda and the Islamic State of Iraq and the Levant (ISIL), which was disowned by al-Qaeda, have endorsed *Ansar Beit al-Maqdis*. In an al-Qaeda video, Zawahiri referred to the group as "our people in Sinai" and showed a funeral for some of its fallen fighters. Zawahiri added that "we must be determined to thwart the Americanized coup in Egypt."[30] Meanwhile, ISIL featured a video of an Egyptian national who fought with them in Syria, urging his fellow Egyptians to take up arms against the Cairo regime. ISIL also featured an Islamic court judge in Syria vowing to support "the mujahedeen in Sinai and the Muslims in Egypt" with "our hearts, our men, and what we can supply you with."[31] In early November 2014, Ansar Beit al-Maqdis swore allegiance to ISIL.[31a] Complicating the picture is that some Egyptian security officials have claimed that Ansar is the Egyptian wing of a Gaza-based salafi jihadist group, though this has not been proven.[32]

In early-2014, one *Ansar Beit al-Maqdis* operative even shot down a military helicopter over the Sinai with a man-portable air defense (MANPAD) system that was probably an SA-16 missile, marking the first time such a missile was used in Egypt by the terrorists, suggesting some obtained training in either Syria or Iraq.[33] *Ansar Beit al-Maqdis* also has taken responsibility for the attacks against security officials and forces in mainland Egypt from September 2013 to the present.

On August 18, 2014, a group calling itself "The Islamic State in Iraq, Syria, and Egypt" claimed responsibility for two attacks earlier in the month in which five policemen were killed. The same group also claimed responsibility for an attack against an Egyptian army post in Farafra in Egypt's Western Desert in July 2014, during which 23 soldiers and officers were killed.[34] However, *Ansar Beit al-Maqdis* also took credit for these same attacks, suggesting Ansar may be capitalizing on the Islamic State's name to sow confusion and to link itself to the militancy of the group that has taken over large swaths of territory in Syria and Iraq.

Other extremist groups in the Sinai include *Tawhid wal Jihad*, an al-Qaeda inspired group believed to have been involved in the 2004-06 terrorist incidents in the Sinai mentioned earlier. Although severely weakened by the large-scale arrests that followed, *Tawhid wal Jihad* is believed by the Egyptian security services to have retained its military wing, though its military commander reportedly was killed by the security forces in January 2014. Other reports suggest that remaining *Tawhid wal Jihad* militants have joined *Ansar Beit al-Maqdis*.[35]

Another group is the Muhammad Jamal Network, named after its leader, Muhammad Jamal, who was first trained by al-Qaeda in the late-1980s. He reportedly has maintained links to Zawahiri as well as al-Qaeda in the Arabian Peninsula and al-Qaeda in the Maghreb. He was imprisoned by the Mubarak regime, released in early-2012 following the revolution, and re-arrested in November 2012 following suspicions that his group was involved in the Benghazi attack on U.S. officials 2 months earlier. It is unknown how large his following is in the Sinai, but there are press reports suggesting that it collaborates with *Ansar Beit al-Maqdis.*[36]

There are some other reports suggesting a presence of the Yemeni-based group, al-Qaeda in the Arabian Peninsula, in the Sinai. In August 2012, CNN, citing an Egyptian security official, claimed that Yemeni militants had come to the Sinai to train local jihadis. In early-September 2013, based on Bedouin sources, Associated Press reported that there had been a recent influx of foreign fighters into the Sinai, including several hundred Yemenis.[37] It is not possible to verify these figures. Egyptian sources believe that while there are probably some foreign Arab fighters in the Sinai, like the Yemenis, the figure of several hundred is probably an exaggeration; the bulk of the fighters are either from mainland Egypt or Bedouin recruits from the Sinai.[38]

In addition to these mainly Egyptian groups, there are unconfirmed reports of Palestinian salafi groups undergoing training in the Gaza Strip and then, after such training, traveling through the underground tunnels to the Sinai where they aid the terrorist cells of such groups as *Ansar Beit al-Maqdis.* This assessment is the view of Egyptian intelligence, according to some press reports,[39] and probably accounts in part for the hostility of the Egyptian security services toward Hamas outside of the Muslim Brotherhood-Hamas connection. It is doubtful that these salafi groups would be able to train in the Gaza Strip without the knowledge of Hamas. One press report noted that Hamas is thought to have an agreement with Mumtaz Dughmush, the head of the Palestinian salafi militant group, *Jaish al-Islam*, which purportedly runs training camps in Gaza for jihadists who subsequently go to fight in Yemen, Syria, and the Sinai.[40] The purported links between the Palestinian salafi groups and the Sinai-based terrorist groups also account for the Egyptian military's clampdown on the tunnels and efforts to seal the border as much as possible.

Transporting Terrorism to the Egyptian Mainland.

More worrisome to the Egyptian government and people has been the violent actions of the Sinai-based terrorist groups to undertake attacks in Cairo and other areas of the Egyptian mainland. In September 2013, Ansar carried out a failed assassination attempt against Egyptian Interior Minister Mohammed Ibrahim.[41] In December 2013, Ansar detonated a large car bomb against the security directorate building in Mansoura, killing 15 people. The following month, it carried out more bombings in Cairo, including one that targeted the Cairo Security Directorate.[42] In late-January 2014, it assassinated a police general and an interior ministry official. Late-January 2014 also witnessed the death of five policemen in the Beni Suef governorate in a firefight with militants.[43]

Although attacks in the Egyptian mainland dropped in February and March, they picked up again in April 2014. Early that month, three bomb blasts took place near Cairo University, killing a senior police officer and wounding at least five other people. The officer was head of the investigations unit of the West Giza district in greater Cairo, suggesting that he was specially targeted. A group called *Ajnad Misr* (Soldiers of Egypt) took responsibility. It was unclear if this was a new group or merely a cell of *Ansar Beit al-Maqdis*, trying to confuse the authorities by using another name. From July 2013 to late-April 2014, according to the Egyptian government, about 500 army personnel, police officers, and officials were killed by the terrorist groups.[44]

Since the summer of 2014, the terrorist groups have also started to attack civilian targets. On June 25, 2014, there were four rudimentary car bomb attacks in the Cairo metro during rush hour. No deaths occurred, but six people were injured. Three days later, an improvised explosive device (IED) was detonated in a building in Giza, south of Cairo, killing a girl and her mother. On July 3, 2014, the anniversary of the removal of Morsi from power, a bomb exploded on a local train in the city of Alexandria, injuring nine people.[45]

It is unclear which group(s) were behind these attacks on ordinary citizens. They were probably designed to sow panic in the general public and to try to turn the public against the military-backed government. The authorities, not surprisingly, blamed the Muslim Brotherhood for the attacks, as it had with previous attacks. Whether the Brotherhood is actually behind such attacks is not known. Some analysts have speculated that since the summer 2013 crackdown on the organization, some younger elements of the Brotherhood, without the guidance from senior officials in the organization, nearly all of whom are now incarcerated, may have joined the actual terrorist groups out of frustration. Some other Brotherhood members, particularly in the summer of 2013, engaged in more rudimentary attacks against police forces and Coptic Churches, usually by hurling Molotov cocktails at such targets.[46] Such attacks differed from the more sophisticated attacks against police targets by *Ansar Beit Al-Maqdis* in December 2013 and January 2014. On July 4, 2014, however, there was a blast at a farm in Fayoum, southwest of Cairo, killing four people who were trying to assemble an IED. The farm was reportedly owned by a Brotherhood activist, suggesting that at least in this case, some Brotherhood members were attempting to engage in violence.[47] In mid-August 2014, the Egyptian authorities accused the Muslim Brotherhood of trying to blow up power line pylons in an effort to exacerbate electricity shortages in Egypt that are affecting millions of families.[48] Again, it is not known whether the Brotherhood was actually behind these attacks or whether this was merely another case of the government's propaganda campaign against the organization.

In the meantime, Ansar has continued to undertake terrorist attacks in the Sinai. For example, in February 2014, it attacked a tour bus of South Koreans in Taba, and it has continued to strike against military targets in the Sinai. On August 20, 2014, four beheaded corpses were found in the town of Sheikh Zuwaid in the Sinai. The victims were believed to have been Sinai residents who were targeted by the extremists for cooperating with the Egyptian police and army.[49] A day earlier, *Ansar Beit al-Maqdis* posted a video online showing the murder of Egyptian soldiers and scenes of an attack on an army checkpoint. The video contained a clip of one of Ansar's leaders admonishing the soldiers for taking up arms for "your leader" (meaning President al-Sissi), who "took the side of the U.S. without hesitation . . ." The soldiers were also admonished for killing "jihadists" and not getting blamed for doing so.[50] Needless to say, such images and video clips have undoubtedly angered the Egyptian military and the public, especially since the military is a largely conscript army.

Egyptian Government's Response in the Sinai.

The Egyptian government has often used brutal methods in the Sinai that have matched at times the brutality of the terrorists. In the summer of 2013, in an example of the latter, terrorists in the Sinai pulled police recruits from buses, laid them on the ground, and shot 25 of them to death.[51] In response to such incidents, the military has often used helicopter gunships to strike suspected militant hideouts in several villages in northern Sinai, killing many people, not necessarily all extremists, in the process. One North Sinai villager told the independent press that military helicopters in the summer of 2013 shelled his village "almost daily" in 1 week. He continued, "Imagine, in 1 week, they bombarded the village with more than a hundred shells."[52] In addition to strikes from the air, the military has also used tanks against Bedouin villages. A villager reported that in September 2013:

> a tank positioned itself in an elevated sandy area and shelled the houses randomly. Most of the residents fled their homes as soon as they heard the sound of tanks, but in one of the homes that had been shelled, we found the bodies of a mother and four children who were killed by the shelling.[53]

In addition, the military reportedly has cut down hundreds of olive trees on the road from El Arish to Rafah in the northern Sinai, presumably to prevent terrorists from using the trees as cover for their own operations against the military but also, in part, as punitive measures against villages suspected of harboring terrorists.[54]

Some villagers in the North Sinai have admitted to journalists "the presence of armed men" in some villages, but said that the military, by using collective punishment on mostly peaceful villagers, is fighting "terrorism with terrorism" and is "creating terrorism" by compelling the disaffected youth to join the extremists.[55] The government has promised that it would compensate villagers to mitigate the effects of such heavy-handed security measures against innocent villagers and their building and crops, but such villagers have reportedly seen no recompense yet.

In 2014, the Egyptian Observatory for Rights and Freedoms issued a scathing report on the Egyptian army's operations in the North Sinai, and characterized the transgressions as "crimes against humanity." The report noted "systematic violations" committed by the military, adding that military operations in the North Sinai alone had left 200 people dead, 1,500 arrested, and destroyed more than 350 houses since July 3, 2013.[56] In addition, on January 25, 2014, 13 Egyptian human rights groups wrote an open letter to the authorities criticizing the excessive force by the military, and calling upon them to employ a more "comprehensive approach" to take into consideration the "economic, social, and political" circumstances of the region, adding that "counterterrorism efforts must not include arbitrary measures but rather be conducted within a framework that respects the law and individual rights throughout the process of identifying the real perpetrators."[57]

Although the government's response has elicited strong criticism from Egypt's human rights community, the Egyptian public, by and large, does not seem to be bothered by such heavy-handed military tactics in the Sinai. First, mainland Egyptians have very few family connections to the Bedouin residents of the Sinai, and second, because of their low opinion of the Bedouins and the prejudices they have toward them, coupled with anger at the terrorist incidents emanating from the Sinai, mainland Egyptians have little sympathy toward the plight of the Bedouins now under siege.[58] In the aftermath of the upsurge in terrorist violence not just in the Sinai but in mainland Egypt, in January 2014, one Egyptian citizen told the press that he would be voting "yes" on the new post-Morsi constitution "because there is a terrorist organization that is trying to destroy us."[59] Another Egyptian citizen said that a vote for the constitution was a vote for al-Sissi, "and Egypt will be safe again."[60] Although such quotes are not a scientific gage of public opinion, they seem to be widely held among many ordinary Egyptians—probably a majority—who harbor negative attitudes toward the Muslim Brotherhood and all Islamist extremist groups, and keenly want stability to return to the country.[61]

The Impact of Renewed Conflict between Israel and Hamas.

The renewed military confrontation between Israel and Hamas that broke out in July 2014 put additional pressure on the Egyptian government and complicated public attitudes toward the Sinai situation.

The government-supported media in Egypt blamed Hamas for the conflict, and charged that the missile strikes by Hamas against Israel and Israel's military retaliation led to the loss of hundreds of Palestinian lives while doing very little damage on Israel. In other words, the pro-government Egyptian media put out the line that Hamas was foolhardy and irresponsible for provoking such a conflict when its outcome was never in doubt. Several pro-government media commentators even made sarcastic remarks about Hamas leader Khaled Mashaal, claiming he was living the life of luxury in Qatar while Palestinians were dying by the hundreds in Gaza because of his foolish policy. One Egyptian commentator stated that he would personally drive Mashaal to the Egyptian-Gaza border and drop him off there so he could perform jihad against Israel—in other words, the commentator was taking Mashaal and other Hamas leaders to task for living in safety while Gaza was in flames and Palestinian civilians were bearing the brunt of the confrontation. Other pro-government television commentators also criticized Hamas for initially rejecting Egypt's efforts to broker a truce and charged that Hamas' demands were unrealistic. One commentator said that one of these demands—having an Arab country (not Egypt) in control of the Rafah crossing point between Gaza and the Sinai, was an affront to Egyptian sovereignty. He added sarcastically that Hamas, by this logic, should simply take over Tahrir Square in downtown Cairo.[62]

Throughout the conflict, Egypt kept the border with Gaza closed, only allowing some wounded Palestinians to come across for medical treatment in Egyptian hospitals. It also allowed for the delivery of some humanitarian supplies to Gaza that was provided by the

Egyptian military. But the Egyptian government was strongly against private Egyptians doing the same. Some opposition party activists signed a petition to President al-Sissi requesting that the government do more. One private convoy of 11 buses and 550 activists was stopped at an Egyptian military checkpoint in the Sinai on the way to Gaza and was told to turn back, supposedly because the military "had security concerns for the safety of the convoy."[63] Another convoy carrying medical supplies and made up of 12 people, including a pharmacist who was a member of the "Popular Campaign to Support the Palestinian Uprising," was able to make it all the way to Rafah by the Gaza border, but not before being stopped by the military at several checkpoints. The medical supplies were then supposed to be picked up by the Palestinian Red Crescent society.[64] It was not clear if the Palestinian Red Crescent Society was able to cross the border to pick up the supplies, or if the Egyptian military transported the supplies to the Red Crescent society on the other side of the border.

As the Gaza conflict dragged on for several weeks in July and the Palestinian civilian death toll mounted, the Egyptian government started to worry about public opinion. While the pro-government Egyptian media did its best to limit the coverage of the conflict and blame Hamas for prolonging it, many Egyptians turned to other media outlets like Al Jazeera television that is owned by the government of Qatar. Although the Egyptian government has tried to de-legitimize Al Jazeera because of its purported support for the Muslim Brotherhood, its more focused coverage of the Gaza conflict may have revived its stock in Egypt.[65]

Not surprisingly, Egyptian supporters of the Muslim Brotherhood tried to stage several demonstrations in mainland Egypt in support of Hamas and the Palestinians of Gaza and against what they saw was the Egyptian government's collusion with Israel to keep Gaza locked up. The government responded forcefully against these demonstrations and arrested many of the participants. Although such measures succeeded in quieting the Egyptian streets, the government was undoubtedly concerned about public opinion and, as a hedge, started to criticize Israel for its military actions in Gaza. This government criticism followed the criticism of some Egyptian commentators who were not affiliated with the Brotherhood and who said that al-Sissi should separate his anger at Hamas from support for the Palestinian people.[66]

Egypt's relationship with the Palestinian issue is very complicated. For decades, Egypt has championed the Palestinian cause and fought several wars ostensibly on behalf of the Palestinians. Most Egyptians sympathize with the Palestinians and hold strong views against Israel despite several decades of peace. These views tend to intensify during periodic conflicts between Israel and the Palestinians.[67] During the late Mubarak period, such as in 2008, many Egyptian citizens—not just Muslim Brotherhood supporters—demonstrated against the Egyptian government for not doing enough to help the Palestinians while an Israeli-Hamas conflict was taking place.[68] During the 2014 conflict between Israel and Hamas, one thoughtful analyst and an expert on Egyptian public opinion noted:

> though many Egyptians view Hamas as an ally of the Muslim Brotherhood, most sympathize with the Palestinians and are angry at Israel. When they see the scale of casualties—for example, the death and destruction in the Shuja'iah neighborhood in Gaza—

they overwhelmingly blame Israel. This is true even as their leaders express anger over Hamas's refusal to accept Egypt's ceasefire proposal.[69]

On the other hand, there have been times, like in 1979 when Egypt was ostracized in the Arab world for signing its peace treaty with Israel, when Egyptians have felt that they have done more than their share for the Palestinian and larger Arab cause, and if the Palestinians and other Arabs do not like it, so be it. Further complicating matters is that Egyptian views toward the Palestinians are not only shaped by periodic Palestinian-Israeli conflicts but by intra-Palestinian politics and the struggles between Hamas and Fatah (the latter in charge of the Palestinian Authority), which tend to be connected to Egypt's own internal political situation.

The Egyptian government under the leadership of Mubarak and now under that of al-Sissi, has long been hostile toward Hamas because of its Muslim Brotherhood connections. Mubarak told a Western journalist in the mid-1990s that:

> this whole problem of terrorism throughout the Middle East is a by-product of our illegal Muslim Brotherhood—whether it's al-Jihad, Hizbollah, in Lebanon, or Hamas. They all sprang from underneath the umbrella of the Muslim Brotherhood.[70]

In the same interview, Mubarak added:

> My own fear is that if there is a delay in the [peace] process, if Arafat fails, all these extremists, all these terrorists trained in Afghanistan, will rush to Gaza and join Hamas. It will be a disaster and cause one hell of a problem for us.[71]

24

Similarly, al-Sissi, since his ouster of Morsi as president in early-July 2013, has put all of the blame for Egypt's terrorist activity at the feet of the Muslim Brotherhood, which the government has declared a "terrorist" organization and has banned its political wing, the Freedom and Justice Party, from participating in elections.[72] Al-Sissi's strategy has been to discredit and weaken both the Brotherhood and Hamas since he believes they feed off each other.

The exception to this hostile position toward Hamas was during the Morsi presidency (2012-13), when Morsi showed sympathy and, at times, expressed solidarity, with Hamas, sent his prime minister to Gaza in a show of solidarity with Hamas during another mini-war with Israel, and even helped to broker a truce between Hamas and Israel in November 2012. Nonetheless, this pro-Hamas position was not shared by the entire government apparatus, which constrained Morsi's actions to some degree. As two scholars have recently noted:

> While one might have thought that Morsi would have opened the floodgates to Hamas, the Brotherhood's ideological bedfellow, in actuality Egypt kept the border with Gaza largely closed during his presidency and continued efforts to destroy tunnels. Whatever his personal sympathies, Morsi stayed within the lines of a policy designed to ensure that Egypt was not stuck holding the Gaza hot potato.[73]

Morsi continued to leave the Sinai/Gaza/Hamas portfolio largely to Egypt's military and intelligence services. He may have wanted to change policy but probably understood that to undercut the military and intelligence services' domination of this portfolio was a bridge too far. He may have also shared the belief, prevalent among Egyptian political elements, that Israel wanted to push the Gaza problem onto the Egyptians.[74] Given Egypt's unhappy experience administering the Gaza Strip from 1948 to 1967, and the mounting issues of overpopulation, poverty, and terrorism in the Gaza Strip, Morsi may not have wanted to take on this headache since he had enough problems in mainland Egypt.

That said, there were always suspicions in Egypt from the Brotherhood's enemies that the Brotherhood was actively conspiring with Hamas. Indeed, within the anti-Brotherhood camp, it is widely believed that Morsi, in jail during the time of the Egyptian revolution in early-2011, had conspired with Hamas to break himself free from prison in Egypt. In fact, this claim has since become one of many official charges that the Egyptian government has leveled against Morsi in his on-again, off-again, criminal trial.[75]

These beliefs of a nefarious Hamas-Brotherhood nexus, however, do not mean that the Egyptian government did not have its own channel to Hamas. Indeed, Egyptian intelligence under Mubarak, which was concerned about divisions among the Palestinians, had long worked behind the scenes to try to bring about a rapprochement between Hamas and its secular Palestinian rival, Fatah.[76] These efforts did not succeed in part because Hamas knew that the Egyptian authorities favored the more moderate Fatah, and did not want to play second fiddle in a unity government.

Ironically, shortly before the outbreak of the latest Gaza conflict in July 2014, such a Palestinian unity government had just come together, at least on paper. It appears that Hamas was compelled to agree to such a unity government in part because it was becoming increasingly isolated in the Arab world.[77] Egypt was not averse to such a unity government because it appeared that Fatah would be the dominant player in it.

However, the Gaza war posed a challenge for al-Sissi because it had the potential to put the Egyptian government in a quandary. Keeping the border with Gaza closed and not allowing significant supplies to enter ran the risk of looking indifferent to the plight of Palestinian civilians, which took the brunt of the Israeli military attacks. On the other hand, the Egyptian government did not want to see Hamas emerge as victor by its firing of hundreds of missiles into Israel and its ability to withstand the Israeli attacks. For this reason, the Egyptian media, as mentioned earlier, went out of its way in characterizing Hamas as reckless and irresponsible for putting the lives of hundreds of thousands of Palestinian civilians in jeopardy.

Unfortunately, there have not been any recent polls in Egypt to gage the reaction of the Egyptian people to what is happening in Gaza, but anecdotal evidence and media monitoring suggests that reactions have fallen largely along the political fault lines that are apparent in Egypt's polarized society between supporters of al-Sissi and supporters of the Muslim Brotherhood. Pro-government citizens, which at this point are probably a majority, sided against Hamas and supported al-Sissi's policies. They tended to believe the government's characterization of Hamas as putting Palestinian civilians in danger, and that Hamas, in conjunction with the Egyptian Muslim Brotherhood, was aiding the terrorism in the Sinai and in mainland Egypt.[78] Even a few pro-government media commentators praised Benjamin Netanyahu and the Israeli army for trying to crush Hamas, (though such statements were probably not shared by the majority of the pro-government supporters).[79] Some Egyptian interlocutors believe that the Egyptians' generally pro-Palestinian position may be changing in the wake of the terrorist threats facing Egypt.[80] The widespread belief among pro-government Egyptians that the Brotherhood and Hamas are out to destroy Egypt by colluding in terrorist acts has apparently affected their view toward the Palestinian cause and has dampened their support for the Palestinian people. Support for the Palestinians (not just Hamas) may have indeed dropped, and we may be witnessing a period similar to what occurred in Egypt after the signing of the Israeli-Egyptian peace treaty in 1979 when an emphasis on Egyptian nationalism prevailed over all other concerns. This anti-Palestinian sentiment, however, is likely to be a passing phenomenon, and once the terrorism problem in Egypt dissipates, there may be a return to the Egyptian people's generally pro-Palestinian position.

Not surprisingly, supporters of the Muslim Brotherhood have been strongly opposed to the Egyptian government's position on Hamas and the Gaza war, have laid the blame on Israel for starting it. They have charged that al-Sissi's government has actively colluded with Israel to punish the Palestinians. Because Egyptian society is so polarized, the Brotherhood (or what is left of the organization after widespread government arrests) would oppose almost anything al-Sissi's government does because it considers that government to be illegitimate and a mortal enemy. But its supporters probably believe these charges, given their ideological outlook. As mentioned earlier, Brotherhood supporters tried to demonstrate in the streets in July 2014 during the Gaza conflict, but such protests were quickly suppressed. They tried to demonstrate again the following month to mark the 1-year anniversary of the government's severe crackdown on the pro-Morsi protestors in August 2013, during which over 600 people died in a single day, but the government suppressed these demonstrations as well.[81]

Because the Egyptian government understands that most Egyptians want stability and an end to terrorism in their own country, it has been trying to conflate Hamas' endangerment of the Palestinian people to the Brotherhood/terrorists' endangerment of the Egyptian people, not to mention what it sees as assistance flowing back and forth between these two extremist groups. This conflation works up to a certain point. However, the government also understands that anti-Israeli sentiment rises among the Egyptian citizens during such periods of conflict in Gaza, and thus it has a vested interest in pushing for a ceasefire to dampen public calls that the government needs to do more to help the Palestinians under siege. Keeping the Sinai border closed to Palestinians (and restricting the shipments of aid to them) over time becomes a problem for the Egyptian government. Although Egypt has other reasons for brokering a cease-fire between Hamas and Israel, namely, returning to an Arab leadership role and undercutting the influence of other regional players,[82] its domestic reasons for wanting the violence to end may be more important.

Although the Gaza conflict ended with a truce, one proposal that has been bandied about is for the Palestinian Authority (under the domination of Fatah) to control Gaza.[83] Such a solution would be welcomed by Egypt and probably by Israel—the latter with qualifications, namely that Hamas should be disarmed and tunnels into Israel from Gaza be completely shut down. Fatah, because of its more moderate position and its close ties to the Egyptian government, would probably be more receptive to Egyptian government calls to shut down the training camps of Palestinian salafi groups who may be aiding extremists in the Sinai. If Fatah were to be in charge of Gaza (even with Hamas' political wing playing a secondary role in the government), Egypt might be amenable to opening the border with Gaza to allow for more goods to be sent and sold there.

However, this optimistic scenario from Egypt's perspective could have unintended consequences. If Fatah were in charge of Gaza and another military confrontation with Israel were to take place (perhaps being initiated by some salafi militant groups in Gaza attacking Israel to embarrass Fatah), Egypt would be even more in a quandary than it is now. Fatah would then have to defend Gaza against a likely Israeli counterattack, and Fatah's police and gendarmerie would be compelled to fight against Israeli forces. Under this scenario, Egypt would not be able to blame Hamas any longer for irresponsible behavior, and whatever blame it might assign to more extreme Palestinian salafi groups for starting such a war, the conflict would soon become a conflict between Fatah and Israel that Egypt would not be able to manage domestically by media manipulation. With Fatah in charge, there would be more calls within the broader Egyptian public to come to the aid of the people in Gaza. Although some elements of the Egyptian government would probably not want to get involved in such a crisis because it has the potential to scuttle the Egyptian-Israeli peace treaty, it might be very difficult for Egypt to keep the Sinai border with Gaza closed under this scenario. And, more ominously for the counterterrorism campaign, there would likely be diminishing support for Egypt's crackdown on the Sinai-based terrorist groups if such groups re-directed their attacks to Israeli targets, especially Israeli soldiers guarding the border. Hence, the old adage of "be careful for what you wish for" may be applicable in this case.

Public Perceptions of the Government's Campaign against Extremists in the Sinai.

As long as the extremists in the Sinai are seen doing damage to the Egyptian state and people—hitting "Egyptian" targets, that is, army, police, and civilians, as well as foreign tourists whose spending provides revenue to the state and helps to employ Egyptian workers—it appears that the majority of Egyptian citizens have no problems with the government's harsh crackdown on the extremists. Moreover, the more the extremists show their true colors by employing brutal tactics against ordinary Egyptian soldiers and people who cooperate with the government, the support for the crackdown is likely to increase. As mentioned earlier, most Egyptians desire stability, and the terrorist attacks in the Sinai and the Egyptian mainland are a threat to this goal. Furthermore, the chaos in Syria and Iraq—especially the military advances and the brutal tactics of ISIL, as well as the instability in Libya next door, makes the Egyptian public even more concerned about terrorism and instability. Most Egyptians do not want to see their country descend into the morass that is now convulsing these and some other countries in the region, especially since Egypt also has a sectarian issue that it needs to manage carefully. About 10 percent of its population are Coptic Christians who have faced sporadic acts of sectarian violence in the recent decades; such violence escalated to high levels during the summer of 2013 when scores of Coptic churches were torched or damaged by supporters of the Muslim Brotherhood who were angry that the Coptic community supported the new government after Morsi was ousted.[84] The Egyptian government under al-Sissi and its supporters, like former foreign minister Amre Moussa, understand these public fears and have used the media to underscore to Egyptian citizens that had al-Sissi not intervened to oust Morsi, "We would have ended up with groups like ISIS doing the same in Egypt."[85] This point is debatable, of course, because there is no way to know for sure whether Morsi was going to lead Egypt to an intolerant state that would support such extremists, but certainly this is how the new government and its supporters are framing the issue, knowing of the public's fear of such a scenario.

For the supporters of the Muslim Brotherhood—which at its peak in 2012 held the allegiance of about a quarter of the population,[86] but has since dropped to an unknown percentile—the government's harsh crackdown in the Sinai is symptomatic of the "illegitimate" military regime that used violence against the Brotherhood in the summer of 2013 and arrested thousands of its leaders, activists, and supporters since that time. In all likelihood, as indicated earlier, the Brotherhood is probably not behind the violence in the Sinai and it denies links to such extremist groups, but it is now more concerned with the self-preservation of its remaining cadres and trying to capitalize on issues where it thinks the government is vulnerable—like closing the Sinai-Gaza border and cooperating with Israel against Hamas. The Brotherhood understands that the Egyptian public is not concerned that some innocent Bedouin villagers are killed in the government's counterterrorism operations because the public's sympathy remains with the military in these operations. The attack by extremists on an Egyptian border outpost in the Western desert that killed 23 Egyptian officers and soldiers elicited broader public anger than the deaths of hundreds of Brotherhood supporters and activists in the summer of 2013, at least among secular-oriented Egyptians.[87]

The chief, outspoken opponents of the government's harsh crackdown in the Sinai are Egypt's human rights activists and a few Sinai Bedouin villagers who have gone to university in the Egyptian mainland. They are the ones who have raised the issue of a counterterrorism campaign that has gone to excesses — some 300 people killed in the Sinai from July 2013 to April 2014, most of whom were civilians[88] — and have provided such information to the independent and foreign press. While it is likely that Egypt's human rights community will continue to raise this issue, which at times becomes an embarrassment for the government, it is unlikely that they will get much traction, given the general public's abhorrence of terrorism and its condescending attitudes toward the Bedouins. As mentioned earlier, the general public's views on government policy toward the Sinai might change if there is a different situation in Gaza — like a war between Fatah and Israel. But barring this scenario, it seems that the human rights community is not going to sway Egyptian public opinion when it issues reports and highlights the government's draconian policies in the Sinai. Hence, it seems that the Egyptian general public has given, and will continue to give, the government wide leeway for its security crackdowns in the Sinai.

Ironically, the institution that might be the most receptive to a change in the Egyptian military's harsh policies in the Sinai may be the Egyptian military itself, or at least elements of the military's officer corps. This potential for a change in policy is not because of the military's kindheartedness toward the Bedouins, nor because of a change in outlook toward the extremists. Rather, it may arise purely out of tactics.[89] The policy of using helicopters and tanks to destroy dozens of homes, hundreds of olive trees, and even whole villages has the potential to backfire by creating more extremist sympathizers and more young disaffected Bedouin youths willing to join the extremist groups. This trend is already underway. While draconian counterterrorism policies may temporarily reduce extremist violence — there was indeed a dip in extremist attacks in the spring of 2014 — such a downward trend is unlikely to last. Indeed, after this dip, extremist violence increased in the summer of 2014. Part of this uptick violence may be because some Egyptian extremists who were fighting in Syria may have returned to Egypt to bring the fight home, but it also may be because new Bedouin recruits from these damaged villages have finished their training with the extremists and are now part of the fight. Countering this trend with more effective policies presents an opportunity for the United States in Egypt.

Recommendations for U.S. Policy.

The evidence presented herein, albeit largely anecdotal, suggests that the vast majority of Egyptians want the terrorism problem of the Sinai to end as soon as possible. If the United States can be of assistance in this process, it would not only help the Egyptian economy rebound because of the likely pick up in tourism and foreign direct investment, it will also help improve bilateral U.S.-Egyptian relations. Even some legal opposition parties in Egypt have indicated privately that if the terrorism problem emanating from the Sinai were to be eliminated, or at least sharply reduced, and U.S. assistance was seen as helpful in this endeavor, the U.S. image in Egypt would greatly improve.[90]

Bilateral U.S.-Egyptian relations hit a low point in 2013 because of the widely held perception in Egypt that the United States aided and abetted Morsi's authoritarian presidency out of some conspiratorial U.S. plan to assist radical Islamists.[91] U.S. criticism of the interim government's harsh crackdown on Morsi's Muslim Brotherhood supporters in August 2013 and the U.S. decision 2 months later to suspend a substantial part of U.S. military assistance package to Egypt, including Apache helicopters, further exacerbated tensions in the relationship. Although most of this assistance has been resumed and relations have rebounded to some degree, tensions still remain.

The key question is how the United States can assist Egypt in its counterterrorism campaign that is most effective and not counterproductive. U.S. policymakers need to emphasize to their Egyptian counterparts the need for a comprehensive approach. This involves persuading Egyptian officials that draconian policies are unlikely to solve the problem. A more effective way to isolate and weaken the terrorist groups in the Sinai is to deny them recruits from the Bedouin villages and deny them safe haven in such villages. Such a policy involves putting more economic resources into the Sinai, providing more jobs for the disaffected Bedouin youths (such as in the tourist towns which heretofore have recruited mostly mainland Egyptians) so they will not rely on smuggling, and changing government policies to recruit Bedouins into a local police force.

Egyptian government officials would need to vet carefully the youth who enter such sensitive positions as policemen and tourist workers to ensure that extremists would not take advantage of such openings and infiltrate these positions.

In addition, a substantial portion of U.S. economic assistance should be channeled to the Sinai to help in job training programs for the Bedouin youths. For example, for Bedouin youths wanting to work in the tourism industry, there could be educational programs to teach languages such as English, French, or German, as well as certain hotel jobs, followed by paid internships in the tourist sector. The United States could also help defray the costs of police training for Bedouin youths.

There is currently a U.S. Agency for International Development (USAID) program in the Sinai called "Livelihood and Income from the Environment" that seeks to help low-income Bedouins living mainly in the central part of the Sinai by promoting projects that are environmentally sustainable. It focuses on such projects as small infrastructure; public transportation systems; and roads, water desalination, and vocational training.[92] While well-intentioned, this program needs to be expanded to include the substantial job training for the tourism industry mentioned earlier, expansion of the program to the northern Sinai region, and more U.S. Government funding. This program has only been funded at $9 million. Given the scope of the problem in the Sinai, it should be funded at a more substantial level, in the range of $50 million per year. Although U.S. economic assistance to Egypt has fallen from an annual $800 million more than a decade-and-a-half ago to about $200 million today, and $50 million for the Sinai might take away from other worthwhile projects that USAID administers in mainland Egypt, a compelling case can be made to the U.S. Congress that an increase in overall U.S. economic assistance to Egypt that would incorporate $50 million for the Sinai is important for U.S. national security interests. Given the increased instability in the Middle East in such countries as Syria, Iraq, and Libya, the U.S. administration would need to emphasize that such an increase in economic assistance to Egypt will help Egypt combat terrorism. Given the fact that the Sinai borders both the Gaza Strip and Israel, the national security argument for such an increase (still small by historical standards) for both human and infrastructure development in the Sinai would be compelling.

Besides persuading the U.S. Congress of the merits of this increased support for the development of the Sinai, U.S. officials also need to persuade Egyptian officials of the program's merits. It is likely that the current USAID program in the Sinai is limited not just because of U.S. financial constraints, but because Egyptian officials are wary about any outside programs in the Sinai Peninsula because it is largely a closed military zone.

There have been discussions among U.S. and Egyptian officials of resuming a bilateral strategic dialogue between the two countries. Such a dialogue was held in the 1990s.[93] Because such a dialogue would be held behind closed doors, sensitive issues could be discussed in this venue outside of the limelight. This would be perfect for U.S. civilian and military officials to discuss the terrorist problem in the Sinai and more effective ways to deal with it. U.S. officials can use the opportunity to discuss the merits of an expanded job training program mentioned earlier as well as the very sensitive issue of creating a local police force made up of Bedouin recruits.

In such a dialogue, U.S. officials should also mention the need to empower Sinai tribal leaders as a hedge against the extremists. Press reports indicate that over the past few years, many of the Bedouin residents have turned to informal Sharia (Islamic law) courts for the adjudication of disputes because the state court system in the Sinai was seen as incompetent and corrupt. In the process, however, these Sharia courts have also undermined traditional Bedouin tribal law known as "urf" which had adjudicated disputes over many centuries. Partly because of the proliferation of the Sharia courts in the Sinai, "the fragmentation of local authorities has been deeply frustrating to tribal leaders seeking the protection of the state."[94] Egyptian officials are well aware of this sentiment but do not seem to have a viable plan to deal with it or take advantage of tribal leaders' resentment of the extremists. U.S. officials can share with their Egyptian counterparts their experiences in Iraq during the "Awakening" in 2007-08 when the United States changed its policy toward the insurgency by reaching out and empowering the Sunni tribes of western and central Iraq to turn against al-Qaeda affiliated extremists.

Recommendations for U.S. Landpower.

U.S. military officials, especially U.S. Army officers, should be an integral part of this strategic dialogue dealing with the terrorist problem in the Sinai. U.S. Army officers who took part in the "Awakening" in Iraq should share their experiences with both Egyptian civilian and military officials. Egyptian officials are very sensitive about outsiders, particularly Westerners, telling them what to do, especially on the security front, and for historical and cultural reasons would not want to be compared with Iraqis. Therefore, U.S. Army officers should approach this issue delicately by way of a briefing, describing what worked and what did not work in Iraq with the Arab Sunni tribes. Moreover, because of the advance of ISIL in Iraq in the summer of 2014 and the need for U.S. and Iraqi officials to approach these Sunni tribes once again to entice them to scuttle their alliance with extremists, U.S. Army officers should also ask their Egyptian counterparts for advice. Such a discussion about Iraq could then lead to a discussion about the Sinai and how to entice the Bedouins there to move away from the extremists, using a more holistic approach.

U.S. Army officers should also bring up Egypt's successful campaign against the violent extremist groups, like the Islamic Group and the *Egyptian Islamic Jihad*, in the 1990s. Egypt first used just the "stick," brute force, against the extremists, but when that did not work, it used both the carrot and the stick. The former involved more development assistance to poor neighborhoods in Cairo and poor rural areas of Upper Egypt, from where the young terrorists came from, and effective propaganda to show that the terrorists were targeting innocent civilians and foreign tourists that hurt Egyptian families trying to make a living.[95] Although Egyptian officials might argue that the Bedouins are different and require a different approach, U.S. Army officers should emphasize that they too found that the carrot and stick approach was indeed more effective in dealing with disaffected tribes.

In addition, the U.S. Army should offer to provide specialized counterterrorism classes to Egyptian military officers at U.S. professional military education institutions. Given that al-Sissi himself was a student at the U.S. Army War College, it is likely that he would approve such training.[96] These specialized classes should emphasize effective ways to seek out and capture extremists in a village without punishing the whole village and creating more extremists in the process.

Coupled with this leadership training, the U.S. Army should offer to train whole Egyptian units involved in counterterrorism operations through joint field exercises, or at a minimum, by specialized U.S. Army trainers. Before being deployed to Iraq, many U.S. Army units practiced counterterrorism techniques in "mock villages" on U.S. military bases that were designed to be as realistic as possible. Training Egyptian army units in such a hands-on way would not only provide them with effective counterterrorism techniques but would move them away from the kind of "scorched-earth" practices they have used so far in the Sinai.

If Egyptian army units would not want to train in the United States, then perhaps they could do so in remote areas of a friendly Arab country like Saudi Arabia, the United Arab Emirates, or Jordan, where U.S. Army trainers could be brought in. Such countries may not be averse to hosting such U.S. training for the Egyptian army provided that it is out of the limelight, because they all have an interest seeing Egypt succeed in its fight against the extremists.

Once these units return to Egypt after their U.S. Army training, there may be a tendency among Egyptian military leaders to say, "Thank you very much, but now we will deal with the terrorists in the Sinai on our own. We know these people, how they think and operate." The danger in this scenario is that the Egyptian military might revert to their usual heavy-handed practices. If such a situation arises, the United

States should use its levers to persuade the Egyptian military to rethink this position and pursue policies that have been learned. If the Egyptian military uses its old practices, such as using U.S. Apache helicopters to attack whole villages as opposed to concentrating on such targets as terrorist camps, the U.S. Army should favor holding up the transfer of spare parts for these helicopters and the delivery of new helicopters. The Egyptian military undoubtedly would react very angrily to this suspension of military assistance, as it has done in the recent past,[97] but using such weapons for indiscriminate attacks against civilians is a tactic that the U.S. Army should counsel its counterparts to cease. Given that the U.S. image in Egypt is still problematic, the U.S. Army should avoid even the appearance of being complicit, even indirectly, in such indiscriminate attacks. This "tough-love" approach would be a strong signal to the Egyptian military that, while the United States "stands by you in your fight against the extremists, there are limits to what we will countenance." Some Egyptian military officers, because they understand that the old ways of dealing with the terrorists are not working, may come to understand the need for the new approach.

Finally, the U.S. military should continue to provide the Egyptian military with sophisticated equipment and intelligence to monitor extremist activity in the Sinai. On August 20, 2002, about 2 weeks after extremists killed 16 Egyptian soldiers along the border with Israel, CNN reported that the Pentagon offered to provide Egypt's army on the Sinai with truck-mounted sensors that provide an electronic signal identifying which nation is operating the vehicle, even from a great distance. The same report stated that the U.S. administration offered Egypt more intelligence sharing, including satellite imagery, drone flights, and intercepts of cell phone and other communications among extremists suspected of planning attacks in the Sinai.[98] Such offers of assistance should continue, not only to help Egypt thwart terrorist attacks, but to underscore the U.S. commitment to Egypt's security. Given the July 2014 attack against Egyptian soldiers in the western desert near Libya, such sophisticated equipment should be offered to the Egyptian army in that region as well.

ENDNOTES

1. Shortly after being sworn in as president, al-Sissi stated: "Defeating terrorism and achieving security is the top priority in our coming phase." See "Sissi Says in First Speech to Nation Fighting Terrorism Will Be Top Priority," *Reuters*, June 8, 2014.

2. In addition, Egyptian authorities have provided overflight and refueling stops for U.S. military aircraft headed to the Persian Gulf region, especially during times of crisis. "Security Assistance: State and DOD Need to Assess How the Foreign Military Finance Program for Egypt Achieves U.S. Foreign Policy Goals," Report to the Committee on International Relations, House of Representatives, Washington, DC: U.S. Government Accountability Office (GAO), April 2006, p. 17.

3. Interviews with Egyptian political analysts, July 2014. See also, Zack Gold, "Security in the Sinai: Present and Future," International Centre for Counter-Terrorism Research Paper, The Hague, The Netherlands, March 2014.

4. "Egypt: Bedouins Begin to Demand Equal Citizenship Rights," IRIN News, June 16, 2011, available from *www.irinnews. org/report/92998/egypt-bedouins-begin-to-demand-equal-citizenship-rights*. See also Vivian Salama, "What's Behind the Wave of Terror in the Sinai," *The Atlantic*, November 22, 2013.

5. For how the 1967 war was seen internally in Egypt, see Steven A. Cook, *The Struggle for Egypt*, New York: Oxford University Press, 2013, pp. 108-129.

6. Abdel Monem Said Aly, "Egypt: A Decade after Camp David," William Quandt, ed., *The Middle East: Ten Years after Camp David*, Washington, DC: The Brookings Institution, 1988, pp. 70-73.

7. "Egypt: Bedouins Begin to Demand Equal Citizenship Rights."

8. Felice Friedson, "Egyptian Editor: Israel Peace Treaty Will Likely be Revised," *Jerusalem Post*, February 27, 2011, available from *www.jpost.com/Middle-East/Egyptian-editor-Israel-peace-treaty-will-likely-be-revised*.

9. Ehud Yaari, "The New Triangle of Egypt, Israel, and Hamas," Washington Institute for Near East Affairs Policy Watch 2193, Washington, DC: Washington Institute for Near East Affairs, January 17, 2014.

10. Jodi Rudoren, "Developments in Iran and Sinai Deepen Israel's Worries about Egypt," *The New York Times*, August 22, 2012.

11. Michele Dunne and Nathan Brown, "How Egypt Prolonged the Gaza War," *Foreign Policy*, August 18, 2014. See also Zack Gold, "Why Israel Will Miss Morsi," *Foreign Affairs*, August 20, 2013, available from *www.foreignaffairs.com/articles/139835/zack-gold/why-israel-will-miss-morsi*.

12. For an examination of the militant groups' ideology and tactics in the 1990s, see Denis Sullivan and Sana Abed-Kotob, *Islam in Contemporary Egypt*, Boulder, CO: Lynne Rienner Publishers, 1999, pp. 71-95.

13. "'Mass Arrests' after Sinai Bombs," BBC News, February 23, 2005. See also Mara Revkin, "Outsourcing Justice in the Sinai: Sharia Courts Thrive in the Shadow of a Weak State," Wordpress, March 11, 2013, available from *mararevkin.wordpress.com/2013/03/11/outsourcing-justice-in-the-sinai-sharia-courts-thrive-in-the-shadow-of-a-weak-state/*.

14. Harriet Sherwood, "Sinai Explodes into Violence after Years of Chronic Poverty and Alienation," *The Guardian*, February 14, 2012, available from *www.theguardian.com/world/2012/feb/14/sinai-violence-poverty-alienation-bedouin-egypt*.

15. Maggie Michael, "Egypt's Sinai Emerges as New Theater for Jihad," Associated Press, September 3, 2013.

16. Gold, "Security in the Sinai."

17. Ehud Yaari and Normand St. Pierre, "Sinai: The New Frontier of Conflict," Washington Institute for Near East Policy Analysis Washington, DC: Washington Institute for Near East Policy, November 20, 2011, available from *www.washington institute.org/policy-analysis/view/sinai-the-new-frontier-of-conflict.*

18. Eric Trager, "Obama's Big Egypt Test: Sinai," *The Atlantic,* January 7, 2013, available from *www.theatlantic.com/international/ archive/2013/01/obamas-big-egypt-test-sinai/266878/.*

19. Ernesto Landano, "Egypt Reacts with Respect to President's New Power," *The Washington Post,* August 14, 2012.

20. "Egypt: Defense Chief Vows to Uproot Militants," *The Washington Post,* August 21, 2012.

21. Revkin, "Outsourcing Justice."

22. "Egypt Charges 200 Islamist Militants with Bombings, Other Violence," *Reuters,* May 10, 2014.

23. Khaled Dawoud, "ISIS at Egypt's Door," Washington, DC: The Atlantic Council, August 20, 2014.

24. Gold, "Security in the Sinai," p. 3.

25. *Ibid.*

26. David Barnett, "The Strategy of Egypt's Ansar Beit al-Maqdis," Washington, DC: The Atlantic Council, February 10, 2014.

27. Revkin, "Outsourcing Justice."

28. Thomas Joscelyn,"Al Qaeda's Expansion in Egypt," Washington, DC: Foundation for Defense of Democracies, February 11, 2014, p. 9, available from *www.defensedemocracy.org/media-hit/ al-qaedas-espansion-in-egypt/.*

29. David D. Kirkpatrick and Eric Schmitt, "Jihadist Return is Said to Drive Attacks in Egypt," *The New York Times*, February 5, 2014.

30. *Ibid*.

31. Dawoud, "ISIS at Egypt's Door"; and Kirkpatrick and Schmitt, "Jihadist Return."

31a. "Egypt's Ansar Bayt al-Maqdis swears allegiance to ISIS: statement," *Al-Ararbiya News*, November 4, 2014, available from *english.alarabiya.net/en/News/middle-east/2014/11/04/Egypt-s-Ansar-Bayt-al-Maqdis-swears-allegiance-to-ISIS.html*.

32. Gold, "Security on the Sinai."

33. David C. Isby, "SAM Used to Down Helicopter over Sinai," *IHS Jane's Missiles and Rockets*, February 11, 2014, available from *www.janes.com/article/33832/sam-used-to-down-helicopter-over-sinai*. See also Zack Gold, "Sinai Security One Year after Morsi," Washington, DC: The Tahrir Institute for Middle East Policy, July 2014, available from *timep.org/esw/articles-analysis/sinai-security-one-year-morsi*.

34. Dawoud, "ISIS at Egypt's Door."

35. Gold, "Security in the Sinai," p. 9.

36. *Ibid*.

37. Maggie Michael, "Egypt's Sinai Emerges as New Theater for Jihad," Associated Press, September 3, 2013.

38. Kirkpatrick and Schmitt, "Jihadist Return." David D. Kirkpatrick and Mayy El Sheikh, "Egypt's Interior Minister Survives Assassination Attempt," *The New York Times*, September 5, 2013, available from *www.nytimes.com/2013/09/06/world/middle-east/egypts-interior-minister-survives-attack.html?_r=0*.

39. Salama, "What's Behind the Wave."

40. Mohammad Daraghmeh, "Leader Says Ranks of Jihadi Fighters in Gaza Rising," *Boston Globe*, March 10, 2014; Salama, "What's Behind the Wave."

41. Kirkpatrick and El Sheikh.

42. Alistair Beach, "Cairo Bomb Attacks: Four Killed and Dozens Wounded on Eve of Revolution Rallies in Egypt," *The Independent*, January 24, 2014, available from *www.independent.co.uk/news/world/africa/cairo-bomb-attacks-four-killed-and-dozens-wounded-on-eve-of-revolution-rallies-in-egypt-9082015.html*.

43. "Five Policemen Killed in Gunmen Attack in Beni Suef," *Al-Masry Al-Youm*, January 23, 2014, available from *www.egyptindependent.com//print/2433774*.

44. "Egyptian Democracy's Death Sentence," *Bloomberg View*, April 28, 2014, available from *www.bloombergview.com/articles/2014-04-28/egyptian-democracy-s-death-sentence*.

45. Zack Gold, "Terrorism Now Targeting Civilians in Egypt," *Terrorism Monitor*, Vol. 12, Issue 16, August 8, 2014.

46. Sarah Sirgany and Laura Smith-Spark, "'Horrible': Christian Churches across Egypt Stormed, Torched," CNN.com, August 16, 2013, available from *edition.cnn.com/2013/08/15/world/meast/egypt-church-attacks/*.

47. Gold, "Terrorism Now Targeting Civilians in Egypt."

48. "Egypt's Power Crisis Worsened by Brotherhood Attacks on Pylons: Interior Ministry," *ahramonline*, August 16, 2014, available from *english.ahram.org.eg/NewsContentPrint/1/0/108572/Egypt/0/Egypts-power-crisis-worsened-by-Brotherhood-attack.aspx*.

49. "Four Beheaded Corpses Found in Egypt's Sinai: Security Sources," *Reuters*, August 20, 2014; "Ansar Bayt al-Maqdis Warns Soldiers of Staying in Army," *Al-Masry Al-Youm*, August 19, 2014, available from *www.egyptindependent.com//print/2438034*.

50. "Ansar Bayt al-Maqdis Warns Soldiers of Staying in Army."

51. Michael, "Egypt's Sinai Emerges."

52. "Sinai Residents Complain of Violations by Egypt Army," *Al-Monitor*, May 7, 2014, available from *www.al-monitor.com/pulse/originals/2014/05/egypt-sinai-war-on-terror-civilians.html*.

53. *Ibid.*

54. Salama, "What's Behind the Wave of Terror."

55. "Sinai Residents Complain of Violations."

56. This report is available from *www.facebook.com/Egypt.O.R.f/posts/1589295377962211?*

57. Gold, "Security in the Sinai," p. 15.

58. Interview with confidential Egyptian sources, August 2014.

59. Erin Cunningham, "Amid Violence, Egyptians Vote on Charter," *The Washington Post*, January 15, 2014.

60. *Ibid.*

61. Abigail Hauslohner, "Many in Egypt Shrug at Loss of Freedoms, Say Stability is Priority," *The Washington Post*, January 9, 2014.

62. These were comments by Egyptian commentator, Osama Mounir, on MEMRI TV on July 17, 2014.

63. "Egypt Medical Aid Convoy Reaches Rafah Crossing," *ahram online*, July 25, 2014.

64. *Ibid.*

65. Shibley Telhami, "The War in Gaza Threatens Egypt too," *Reuters*, July 22, 2014.

66. Rana Harbi, "Egyptian Media Wages Incitement Campaign against Palestinians as Gaza Burns," *Al-Akhbar*, July 18, 2014.

67. Telhami, "The War in Gaza."

68. Per Bjorklund, "Egypt Government Feels Its People's Ire," *The Electonic Intifada*, January 5, 2009, available from *electronic intifada.net/content/egypt-government-feels-its-peoples-ire/7925*.

69. Telhami, "The War in Gaza."

70. Mary Ann Weaver, "The Novelist and the Sheikh," *The New Yorker*, January 30, 1995.

71. *Ibid.*

72. The Muslim Brotherhood was officially declared a terrorist organization by the Egyptian government in December 2013. In August 2014, its political wing, the Freedom and Justice Party, was banned from participating in elections.

73. Dunne and Brown, "How Egypt Prolonged the War."

74. *Ibid.* See also Telhami, "The War in Gaza."

75. Erin Cunnigham, "Egyptian Police Official Slain; Ousted President Appears in Court," *The Washington Post*, January 20, 2014.

76. "Palestinian Reconciliation: A History of Documents," *Al Akhbar*, April 28, 2014, available from *english.al-akhbar.com/node/19580*.

77. Peter Beaumont, "Fatah and Hamas Agree on Palestinian Prime Minister," *The Guardian*, May 29, 2014, available from *www.theguardian.com/world/2014/may/29/fatah-hamas-agree-new-palestinian-prime-minister*.

78. Mohannad Sabry, "Hatred of Hamas Leaves Egyptians Unsympathetic," *Al-Monitor*, July 14, 2014, available from *www. al-monitor.com/pulse/originals/2014/07/hamas-egypt-hate-gaza-no-sympathy.html*.

79. Harbi.

80. *Ibid*.

81. "Egyptian Police Kill Five Anti-Government Protestors," *Alalam*, August 16, 2014.

82. Tim Lister, "Egypt Reclaims Role as Arabs' Indispensable Nation with Gaza Talks," *CNN.com*, August 7, 2014.

83. For an American perspective on this idea, see Samuel R. Berger and Stephen J. Hadley, "The Palestinian Authority should return to Gaza," *The Washington Post*, August 21, 2014.

84. Sirgany and Smith-Spark.

85. Dawoud, "ISIS at Egypt's door."

86. During the first round of the presidential elections in 2012, in which there were several candidates with different ideological persuasions and affiliations, Mohammed Morsi, the Muslim Brotherhood candidate, received about 25 percent of the vote. This percentile is roughly what some Egyptian political scientists have in the past claimed was the Brotherhood's support in the population. Because of dissatisfaction with Morsi's presidency and the government's media campaign against the Brotherhood, actual support for the organization is probably much less today.

87. The Egyptian government declared 3 days of mourning for the fallen soldiers. "Egypt Army Reveals Details of Al-Wadi Al-Gedid Deadly Attack on Soldiers," *ahram online*, July 22, 2014. See also Eric Trager and Gilad Wening, "Egypt's Western Security Concerns," Washington Institute for Near East Policy Watch 2301, Washington, DC: Washington Institute for Near East Policy, August 8, 2014.

88. Michele Dunne and Scott Williamson, "Egypt: Counterterrorism and the Politics of Alienation," Washington, DC: Carnegie Endowment for International Peace, August 20, 2014.

89. Interestingly, al-Sissi seems to recognize the risks of pursuing draconian policies in the Sinai. He stated in an interview:

"We don't want killing of innocents so that won't become an excuse for the expansion of these operations [in the Sinai]. That's what makes it go on. . . ." See "Text of Sissi interview with Reuters," *Reuters*, May 15, 2014.

90. This comment was made to the author from an Egyptian opposition party leader in April 2014.

91. Abigail Hauslaohner, "Egyptian Group Accuses US of Keeping Morsi in Power," *The Washington Post*, June 30, 2013.

92. Available from *www.usaid.gov/egypt/environment-and-global-climate-change*.

93. The "Strategic Dialogue," which started under the Clinton administration, was at the ministerial level. It grew out of the "Gore-Mubarak Partnership" that aimed to enhance and promote commercial relations between Egypt and the United States in the 1990s.

94. Revkin, "Outsourcing Justice."

95. For example, the government spent considerable money to improve the Imbaba neighborhood in Cairo, which, in the early-1990s, was considered a hotbed for Islamic Group militants.

96. As Defense Minister, al-Sissi called for expanded counterterrorism training for the military and considered the establishment of a rapid response, counterterrorism unit. See Gold, "Sinai Security One Year after Morsi."

97. Julian Pecquet, "Obama Administration Holding Up Apache Helicopters to Egypt," *Al-Monitor* June 3, 2014, available from *www.al-monitor.com/pulse/originals/2014/06/egypt-helicopters-apaches-hold-up-leahy-obama.html*.

98. Barbara Starr, "Panetta Tries to Help Secure Sinai with Intel Aid," CNN, August 20, 2012, available from *security.blogs.cnn.com/2012/08/20/panetta-tries-to-help-secure-sinai-with-intel-aid/*.